2/04

César E. Chávez

A Proud Heritage The Hispanic Library

César E. Chávez

The Fight for Farm Workers' Rights

Ann Gaines

Published in the United States of America by The Child's World®
PO Box 326 • Chanhassen, MN 55317-0326 • 800-599-READ • www.childsworld.com

Acknowledgments

The Creative Spark: Mary Francis-DeMarois, Project Director; Carrie Nichols Cantor, Series
Editor; Robert Court, Design and Art Direction
Carmen Blanco, Curriculum Adviser
The Child's World®: Mary Berendes, Publishing Director

Photos

AP/Wide World Photos: 19, 30; Bettmann/CORBIS: cover, 34; Bob Parent/Archive Photos:
32; CORBIS: 11, 13; Jonathan Blair/CORBIS: 25; César Chávez Foundation: 16, 22; Farrell
Grehan/CORBIS: 27, 28; Hulton-Deutsch Collection/CORBIS: 35; Library of Congress: 13;
Christine Osborne/CORBIS: 15; Walter P. Reuther Library, Wayne State University: 7, 9, 20,
33; James A. Sugar/CORBIS: 12

Library of Congress Cataloging-in-Publication Data
Gaines, Ann.
César E. Chávez : the fight for farm workers' rights / by Ann Gaines.
p. cm. — (A proud heritage. The Hispanic library)
Summary: Traces the life and accomplishments of Mexican American labor leader
César Chávez, who founded the United Farm Workers union to promote better wages and
working conditions for migrants and other farm workers.
Includes bibliographic references and index.
Contents: A hard beginning—Learning to organize—The grape boycott—The movement
grows—Timeline.
ISBN 1-56766-209-9 (Library Bound : alk. paper)
1. Chavez, Cesar, 1927——Juvenile literature. 2. Mexican Americans—Biography—Juvenile
literature. 3. Labor leaders—United States—Biography—Juvenile literature. 4. United Farm
Workers—History—Juvenile literature. [1. Chavez, Cesar, 1927– 2. Labor leaders. 3. Mexican
Americans—Biography. 4. Migrant labor. 5. United Farm Workers.] I. Title. II. Proud heritage
(Child's World (Firm))
HD6509.C48G34 2003
331.88'13'092—dc21
[B]   2002152664

Chapter One

A Hard Beginning

The young César Chávez (SAY-zar SHAH-vezz) started out with almost nothing. As **migrant** farm workers, he and his family led a hard life. They spent long hours doing backbreaking work for very little money. César never had much of an education, yet he grew up to be a powerful man. By founding a **union** for farm workers, he improved the lives of thousands of poor people. He inspired many people, especially Mexican Americans, to fight for the right to be treated fairly.

New Home, New Farm

César Chávez's family came from Mexico. In the 1880s, his grandfather, Césario Chávez, was having trouble earning enough money to feed his family. He decided it was time to leave Mexico and **emigrate** to the United States.

There the Chávez family settled in Arizona, where they fared much better. The government was giving away large areas of land. Césario Chávez claimed a **homestead** of 160 acres (65 hectares) near the city of Yuma that became the family's new farm. They grew crops and raised animals to eat as well as sell.

César Chávez spent much of his childhood on a farm near Yuma, Arizona, the remains of which are shown here.

César Chávez's father, Librado Chávez, was just two years old when his family moved to the United States. One of 15 children, he grew up working next to his father. After his marriage to a woman named Juana, he started his own business. About 20 miles (32 kilometers) north of Yuma he opened a grocery store. Later he opened an auto repair shop and a pool hall next door.

Librado and Juana Chávez had six children. When their second son, César Estrada Chávez, was born on March 31, 1927, the family was doing well. A close and happy group, they spent a lot of time with César's grandmother, grandfather, aunts, and uncles. They also had many friends. Librado let many people who lived near them take things from his store and pay for them later.

Difficult Years

When the **Great Depression** began in 1929, things changed. Many of the people to whom Librado had sold things could not pay him what they owed. And the family had another problem. Librado had borrowed money to buy 40 acres (16 hectares) of land next to his store. He lost that land when he could not make the payments on it. He had also fallen behind on paying land taxes. He had to sell his store.

By this time Césario Chávez had died. But Librado's mother, whom the family called Mama Tella, still lived on their farm. Almost 100 years old, she invited Librado's family of five—he and Juana had three children then and would soon have a fourth—to live with her in her old adobe house. Librado, Juana, and the children all pitched in and worked the farm. They never had much money, but they had enough to eat. Looking back on this time, César remembered feeling content.

César learned a lot from his family members. They passed on their willingness to work hard. One thing his mother, in particular, taught him was to care for those less fortunate than him. During the Depression of the 1930s, many men lost their jobs. They tramped all over,

In 1942, César Chávez is dressed for his eighth-grade graduation and holds his diploma in his right hand.

looking for work. Juana Chávez fed everybody who came to their door.

While living with Mama Tella, César Chávez and his siblings attended public school, but they were not happy there. Although they learned a lot at home, they had less success at school. Their family always spoke Spanish at home, and César learned to read when he was little. But he did not know much English. At school, teachers hit Mexican American children with a ruler whenever they spoke Spanish. Schoolmates teased them because they spoke with an accent.

In 1937, things got worse for the Chávez family. The family owed more than $4,000 in taxes on Césario's homestead. The U.S. government had a loan program to help families in their situation. But a banker who wanted their land cheated them, saying they could not have a loan. The state of Arizona then took away their land. To buy it back, they would have to come up with the money they owed.

Desperate to earn money, Librado had already left his family and gone to California to find work. He became a migrant, or seasonal, farm worker. Farmers would hire migrant workers for a short time to plant or harvest a single crop. They paid them a small amount of money. After a couple of weeks, when the job was done, the workers had to move on.

Migrant farm workers lived in labor camps, which were usually shacks, built of wood and tar paper, owned by the farmers. They had no indoor plumbing. Some had no electricity. Living out in the country, the workers had to buy food and other supplies from stores run by the farmers. Prices at these stores were very high. Migrant workers received little pay and had high living expenses. As hard as they worked, they barely earned enough to eat.

Migrant farm workers lived together in camps. Their houses were rundown shacks with no running water.

Uprooted

Eventually the Chávez family realized it would be impossible to earn enough money to buy back their homestead. Juana and the children followed Librado to California. Looking back, César Chávez remembered, "When we left the farm, our whole life was upset, turned upside down. We had been part of a very stable community, and we were about to become migrant workers. We had been uprooted."

From this point on, life was very hard for the Chávez family. A contractor hired them to pick grapes. The contractor worked for a rich man who owned a vineyard. When the work was done, Librado went to the contractor's house to collect their pay,

Like this worker at a Windsor, California, vineyard, the Chávezes picked grapes for a living.

A typical house for farm workers was made of rough wood and tin cans from the garbage.

only to discover that he had moved away. There was nothing for the Chávezes to do but move on.

As the seasons changed, they moved from one place to another, harvesting different crops. In the winter, there was no work. Sometimes the Chávez family managed to save enough money to rent a house during the winter. They usually found one in a **barrio** called Sal Si Puedes (which means "Get Out If You Can") in San Jose. One winter they had to live in a tent. They cooked their food on a big metal can in which they burned whatever dry wood they could find.

Through these difficult times, Librado and Juana Chávez hoped to improve their family's life. Whenever they had enough money, the children didn't work full-time but went to school instead. Over the years, César Chávez went to 30 schools, each for only a few weeks or, at most, a few months. He never liked any of them.

No matter where they went, the Chávez children, like other Mexican Americans, faced discrimination. Once, a teacher made César wear a sign that said, "I am a clown. I speak Spanish." The fact that the family was always on the move only made matters worse. If they had been able to stay in one place, their teachers might have had time to find out that they were, in fact, smart and capable.

New Experiences

César Chávez finally quit school altogether after he finished the eighth grade. He learned only from his friends and family or by himself.

When he was 12 years old, he learned about something that would change his life. His family was living in a migrant camp near San Jose in northern California, where some union people were trying to organize farm workers. Workers join unions because, by coming together as a large group, they are able to demand better treatment.

Farm workers labored for long hours at backbreaking work under the hot sun.

The union in San Jose promised to help the workers fight for fair pay and better working conditions. Its leaders organized a **strike.** Workers who were members of the union refused to go to work until farmers agreed to treat them better. Librado Chávez joined the union and walked the **picket lines.**

But the strike was quickly broken. The farmers refused to meet the workers' demands. Disappointed, the workers had to go back to the fields or let others take their jobs.

César always remembered both the hope and the disappointment the workers felt. Over the years, he watched his father join different unions, including the Tobacco Workers, the Cannery Workers, the National Farm

Young César Chávez served in the U.S. Navy from 1946 to 1948.

Labor Union, and the Packing House Workers. All of these groups were small and lacked the power to change the system.

As a teenager, César Chávez became rebellious. He became a *pachuco*. Pachucos were Mexican boys who belonged to the gangs that grew up in California's largest cities. Some members were only mildly rebellious, like César. They might speak disrespectfully to grown-ups, for example. Others were violent and robbed stores. They wore what they thought were very cool clothes, including zoot suits and porkpie hats, and they talked in slang. Their behavior and dress outraged many Anglos who expected Mexican Americans to be respectful toward them. In 1943, in Los Angeles and elsewhere, soldiers, sailors, and policemen attacked "zoot-suiters."

The Chávez family was relieved when, in 1946, César joined the U.S. Navy. After he went through basic training in San Diego, he was sent to the South Pacific. César found that the navy discriminated against Mexican

Americans (as well as other minorities). Navy officers gave them low-ranking jobs and refused to promote them. César's stint in the navy ended in 1946. Then he returned home to his family in California.

Mexican Immigration

Some 150 years ago, most Mexican Americans were not immigrants. They hadn't moved—the border had! When Texas declared its independence from Mexico in 1836, the Mexicans who lived there became citizens of the Republic of Texas. Ten years later, they became Americans when Texas became a state. After the Mexican War (1846–1848), the United States claimed the lands that are now called Arizona, Nevada, California, and Utah, as well as parts of New Mexico, Colorado, and Wyoming. Mexicans living in these areas became citizens of the United States.

When the Mexican Revolution began in 1909, many more Mexicans moved to the United States. Since then, the Mexican American population of the United States has grown steadily. Today, 43 million Mexicans cross the border every year. Some come legally. Others, desperate for work, break the law by sneaking into the country.

Chapter Two

Learning to Organize

Back at home, César Chávez returned to working in the fields. In 1947, he went out on strike for the first time. It was a cotton workers' strike organized by the National Farm Labor Union. The strike ended successfully after two weeks, when the workers received a pay raise. Chávez and the other workers were proud. Farm workers' unions had won few strikes in the past. Chávez hoped to take part in more strikes. One day, in fact, he hoped to become a decisionmaker in a union and help organize a strike.

César Chávez worked alongside his family in the fields for one more year. Then, in 1948, he married another migrant worker named Helen Fabela. He and Helen had known each other for five years. Now husband and wife, César and Helen picked grapes for a while and then cotton. The first of their eight children,

People visit the former Chávez home in Oxnard, California, to pay respect to César Chávez and all that he accomplished.

Fernando, was born in 1949. The youngest, Anthony, was born in 1958.

César, along with one of his brothers and a cousin, took jobs in a lumber company in Crescent City. In 1952, they moved to San Jose, where César worked in another lumber mill. There he and Helen lived in his old neighborhood, the barrio Sal Si Puedes. In San Jose, César and Helen Chávez spent some time teaching farm workers from Mexico to read and write English so that they could take a test to become American citizens.

César Chávez and his wife, Helen, had eight children. Pictured here are six of them (from left to right beginning in the front row): Paul, Liz, Anthony, Anna, Eloise, and Sylvia.

New Friends, New Job

Chávez became friends with a local priest named Donald McDonnell. When McDonnell went to labor camps and the county jail to hold church services, Chávez went along and helped him. In turn, McDonnell gave him books to read. Chávez read about Mohandas Gandhi, a great leader from India who helped his country overthrow its bad government through peaceful means. Chávez also became interested in how unions worked and what made them succeed. McDonnell, who had long been interested in helping migrant workers, told him all he knew about the history of farm workers in California.

Through McDonnell, Chávez met another man who influenced him greatly. Fred Ross had come to Los Angeles and started a group called the Community Service Organization (CSO). Its aim was to organize poor people, register them to vote, give them free education, and help them fight for their **civil rights.** Ross was forming new CSO chapters in other California cities. In San Jose, he met McDonnell. When he asked the priest to recommend Mexican Americans who would be good CSO leaders, McDonnell gave him Chávez's name.

Chávez did not want to meet Ross. He thought American "do-gooders" could not really help Mexican Americans or farm workers. Ross went to the Chávez

Chávez worked for the Community Service Organization (CSO) for ten years. This photo shows CSO members urging people to vote on Election Day. César Chávez is on the far right.

home and met Helen. She liked him and told him where to find her husband. Much to César's surprise, he liked Ross too. The two men became friends.

Chávez went to work for the CSO. At first he registered people in his neighborhood to vote. Later he set up a service center where poor people could go for legal advice, such as when they had trouble with their landlord.

Chávez worked for the CSO for ten years, beginning in 1952. Eventually he was put in charge of all the group's

California chapters. Because of his job, his family continued to move often. The moving was hard, but working for the CSO was good for Chávez. It taught him how to organize people and how to speak in public. It also allowed him to meet leaders of other organizations that helped poor people, Mexican Americans, and farm workers.

"The Cause"

Chávez wanted the CSO to begin a big effort to organize farm workers and form a union. Other leaders in the organization did not agree. In 1962, at age 35, Chávez resigned. He had decided to form a farm workers' union by himself. He and Helen moved their family to the town of Delano, in California's San Joaquin Valley. Because farms and ranches surrounded the town, a large number of farm workers lived there year-round.

The Chávez family had a little money saved but not nearly enough to live on for any length of time. Helen went back to working in the fields. César worked part-time, but he devoted most of his time to organizing his union. Chávez started to travel to the camps where farm workers lived. As he went, he gave out questionnaires asking the workers what they wanted a union to do for them. Everywhere he went he gained some followers. Other members of his family helped as well.

After six months, on September 30, 1962, Chávez was able to gather 150 delegates and their families—about 300 people altogether—in Fresno, California. It was the first meeting to organize what was named the National Farm Workers Association (NFWA). At this meeting the delegates voted for union officers. Chávez was elected president. They also approved their flag, a red background with a black eagle in a white circle in the center. They adopted "La Causa" (The Cause) as their motto. They decided membership dues would be $3.50 per month.

Long before this meeting, Chávez had made some important decisions. He knew that in the past, people who had tried to form strong farm workers' unions had made the same mistake over and over again. They tried to hold strikes before they had organized their members. He decided to be more patient. He would make sure his organization was strong before staging any strikes.

In the months that followed NFWA's first meeting, its membership grew. The union started to offer its members more and more services. Chávez organized a credit union, where members could start savings accounts and borrow money. The union started a newspaper, called *El Malcriado* ("The Unruly One").

By 1964, the NFWA had 1,000 members. Its main office in Delano had been built by volunteers with donated materials. Chávez, who got a salary of $50 per month, had an office there. His family remained poor, but they were happy. Chávez had high hopes that the union would begin to bring about positive changes in farm workers' lives.

Chávez's hoped his work would make life better for many hardworking farm families.

Chapter Three

The Grape Boycott

César Chávez spent three years setting up the NFWA. Then, in 1965, he felt it was time to use its muscle to fight for workers' rights.

That year Mexican American and Filipino grape pickers, who were being paid no more than $1.25 per hour, learned that the U.S. government was allowing farmers to bring in workers from Mexico. They were paying the workers $1.40 per hour. A small farm workers' union, the Agricultural Workers Organizing Committee—whose members were mostly Filipinos—staged a strike and won a pay raise for all grape pickers.

When this same group went on strike again later that fall, Chávez and the members of his NFWA joined them. Thousands of workers went out on strike. They organized picket lines. **Scabs** crossed their lines to work in the fields. Vineyard foremen swore at them, sprayed them with pesticides, and threatened them with dogs and shotguns.

Following instructions from Chávez, the NFWA strikers did not respond with violence. They remained peaceful even when the police sided with the vineyard owners and arrested picketers for disturbing the peace.

Strikers and their families suffered incredible hardships without their paychecks. They could not afford to buy

In 1965, Mexican American grape pickers voted to go on strike in Delano, California.

In 1966, Mexican American grape pickers hold signs for their cause. Being on strike can be hard work.

food, clothing, or shoes. Despite these difficulties the strike continued. In fact, it grew.

Support throughout the Nation

The 1960s was a time of great change in the United States. President Lyndon B. Johnson, proposing what he called the Great Society, asked Americans to dedicate themselves to fight poverty. At the same time, many Americans had begun to protest racism all across the country. A great movement—the civil rights movement—

was underway. A **Chicano** movement had also begun, with Mexican Americans fighting discrimination.

Believing in equality for all, many Americans saw that farm workers were being treated unfairly. Volunteers by the hundreds came to support the strikers. Many were clergy—ministers, priests, and rabbis. Others were university students. The evening news began to cover the story. Many people started to **boycott** grapes, refusing to buy them until farmers agreed to treat their workers better.

In March 1966, Chávez organized a march of strikers and their supporters to Sacramento, the capital city of California. In 25 days, he and hundreds of others walked 250 miles (400 kilometers) to show their dedication to the cause.

The march did not change the minds of the growers, but it did catch the attention of California's governor, Edmund G. Brown. He began to work with the legislature to pass new laws protecting the rights of farm workers, particularly their right to form unions. As a result of the march, Chávez became famous across the country.

In 1966, the National Farm Workers Association changed its name to the National Farm Workers Union (NFWU). Later that same year, another union called the Agricultural Workers Organizing Committee and the NFWU merged to form a single new union called the United Farm Workers (UFW). César Chávez was elected its president.

In 1968, César Chávez called on Americans to boycott grapes. In this photograph from 1969, Chávez carries a sign in front of a supermarket in Seattle, Washington.

Even so, the owners refused to meet the demands of the workers for four more years. They kept expecting the workers to give in and go back to work. But César Chávez continued to encourage the strikers to hold out, saying, "We know we will win in the end; we learned many years ago that the rich may have money, but the poor have time."

To bring attention to the strike, Chávez twice fasted for long periods of time. His hunger strikes made the news. Inspired in large part by Chávez's words and example, the workers remained on strike.

Meanwhile, more and more Americans started boycotting grapes to support the strikers. Farmers made less money because they were selling fewer grapes each year. Finally, in 1970, the first of the grape growers signed new contracts with the union. They agreed to raise workers' wages and support their union. The union declared an end to the boycott, and its members went back to work.

Chapter Four

The Movement Grows

César Chávez was glad when the grape strike ended. But he knew his work was not yet done. He immediately turned his attention to other problems that farm workers faced. The same year the grape boycott ended, he called for a nationwide boycott of lettuce because lettuce pickers were not getting fair pay. People who sympathized with the cause of the farm workers refused to buy lettuce. Some even picketed in front of supermarkets.

In 1973, the agreements between the grape pickers' and their employers expired. Chávez and other union members were not happy with the new contract the growers offered. Chávez then organized a second grape boycott that lasted for two years. It was a great success. A survey showed that 17 million Americans refused to buy grapes.

Over time, Chávez and the union he had founded brought about more improvements in the lives of migrant farm workers. Workers were able to work fewer hours under better conditions and for higher pay.

Chávez's life changed too. Over the years, he came to be seen as one of the most successful of all American labor leaders. He also gained fame as a leader of Mexican Americans. For almost 20 more years, UFW members continued to elect him as their president.

In the early 1970s, César Chávez and Coretta Scott King, the widow of Rev. Martin Luther King Jr., led a boycott march in New York City.

Back to Arizona

In 1993, Chávez went back to Arizona, the state where he was born. A giant company called Bruce Church Inc., which grew lettuce and other vegetables in California, was suing the UFW. Church took the union to court, demanding that its members pay millions of dollars in damages it claimed had resulted from a UFW boycott of its lettuce during the 1980s.

This poster from the late 1970s urged people not to buy grapes or lettuce.

Chávez went there to help other UFW leaders and lawyers prepare their case. He began a hunger strike, hoping to gain the attention of the media.

After nine days, on April 23, 1993, he ended his strike. That night he died of natural causes, peacefully in his sleep, at the age of 66.

The death of César Chávez made headlines all over the world. Six days after his death, his funeral was held in Delano, California. Thousands joined in a march behind

his casket. President Bill Clinton issued a proclamation about Chávez, saying:

With natural leadership and unflagging determination, he achieved real progress where others had failed. . . . He focused our nation's attention on the economic and social plight of migrant farm workers and, in the process, taught us how injustice anywhere affects us everywhere.

In 1987, Chávez worked hard to ban the use of five pesticides linked to cancer, birth defects, and other illnesses.

A man named Arturo Rodriguez became president of the UFW in 1994. But the UFW has continued to honor the memory of César Chávez, declaring its intent to "continue along the path begun by César Chávez. La Causa continues."

Fifty years earlier, migrant farm workers had no strong union to protect them or help them negotiate with employers. Now their situation is very different. They make more money and work under better conditions, thanks to the lifelong efforts of César Chávez.

Remembering César Chávez

Since his death, people have found many ways to honor César Chávez. On August 8, 1994, his family was invited to the White House to attend a ceremony, where President Bill Clinton awarded him the U.S. Medal of Freedom. One month later, the governor of California, Pete Wilson, signed a new law declaring César Chávez's birthday, March 31, a state holiday. Celebrations are also held in his honor elsewhere in the country on that day. Today all over the United States there are streets, schools, libraries, and parks named after this great man.

1927: César Chávez is born on March 31.

1937: The Chávez family loses its farm during the Great Depression. They become migrant farm workers.

1944–1946: César Chávez serves in the U.S. Navy in the Pacific.

1947: Chávez joins the National Farm Labor Union.

1948: Chávez marries Helen Fabela.

1949: Fernando Chávez is born, the first of César and Helen's eight children.

1952: Chávez goes to work in San Jose for the Community Service Organization (CSO). He remains there for ten years.

1962: Chávez leaves the CSO after its leaders decide they cannot help farm workers organize a union. He starts his own farm workers' union, the National Farm Workers Association. This later becomes the National Farm Workers Union.

1965: After Filipino grape pickers in Delano, California, go on strike for higher wages, Chávez's union joins the strike against grape growers.

1966: In March, Chávez and 70 strikers begin a march to Sacramento to drum up support for the union. By the time they reach the state capital on April 11, they number 10,000.

The National Farm Workers Union and the Agricultural Workers Organizing Committee join forces to form the United Farm Workers (UFW).

BUY UNION

1968: Chávez begins a 25-day fast to gain support for nonviolence in union organizing efforts. Later in the year, he announces his plans for a consumer boycott of California grapes. In July more than 100 grape growers and shippers sue Chávez and the UFW, claiming $25 million in losses because of the boycott.

1970: The UFW and most major grape growers reach contract agreements. Chávez starts a boycott of lettuce.

1988: Chávez fasts for 36 days to protest pesticide use in California.

1990: Mexican president Salinas de Gortari awards Chávez the Aguila Azteca, the highest Mexican civilian award, because of his service to Mexican migrant farm workers who work in the United States.

1993: Chávez dies of natural causes in San Luis, Arizona, on April 23. He had gone there to help his union defend itself against a lawsuit. To bring attention to the lawsuit, he had gone on a hunger strike.

1994: President Bill Clinton awards the U.S. Medal of Freedom to Chávez. California governor Pete Wilson declares Chávez's birthday a state holiday.

Arturo Rodriguez takes over as president of the UFW.

barrio (BAR-ree-oh) In the United States, city neighborhoods where most of the residents speak Spanish are called barrios. The Chávez family lived in a barrio in San Jose, California.

boycott (BOY-kott) People boycott something when they refuse to buy it. César Chávez convinced people across the nation to boycott grapes in order to support the farm workers' demands for higher pay.

Chicano (chih-KAH-noh) A Chicano is a Mexican American. Mexican Americans began using the word *Chicano* in the 1960s to express pride in their heritage.

civil rights (SIV-il RYTZ) Civil rights are people's rights to freedom and equal treatment. In the 1960s, a civil rights movement fought to win fair, equal treatment for African Americans and other minorities.

emigrate (EH-mih-grayt) To emigrate is to move from one country to another. Chávez's grandparents emigrated from Mexico to the United States.

Great Depression (GRAYT dih-PREH-shun) The Great Depression was a worldwide economic collapse in the 1930s when many companies closed down and farms failed. During the Great Depression, many Americans were out of work and had little money.

homestead (HOME-sted) Under a government program, settlers in the American West received homesteads, pieces of land, simply by settling on them. César Chávez's grandfather was one of many who claimed a homestead in Arizona.

migrant (MY-grent) A migrant is a person who moves from place to place. Migrant farm workers work on various farms throughout the year.

picket lines (PIK-it LYNZ) Picket lines are lines of protesters who carry signs near a place of business. Grape pickers would often form picket lines in the vineyards where they normally worked.

scabs (SKABZ) Scabs are people employers hire to replace striking workers. If employers hire scabs to replace striking workers, then the strikers might not get their jobs back.

strike (STRYK) Workers stage a strike by refusing to work until their employer agrees to certain demands. Chávez directed many strikes by farm workers.

union (YOON-yen) A union is an organization of workers. Workers join unions because, by uniting into large groups, they are better able to fight for pay increases, shorter work weeks, and benefits.

Books

Altman, Linda Jacobs. *Amelia's Road*. New York: Lee and Low, 1993.

Atkin, S. Beth. *Voices from the Fields: Children of Migrant Farmworkers Tell Their Stories*. New York and Boston: Little, Brown & Co., 1993.

Concord, Bruce W. *César Chávez, Union Leader*. Bromall, Pa.: Chelsea House Publishers, 1992.

Jiménez, Francisco. *Breaking Through*. Boston: Houghton Mifflin, 2001.

Jiménez, Francisco. *The Circuit: Stories from the Life of a Migrant Child*. Boston: Houghton Mifflin, 1999.

Wade, Linda R. *The Mexican Americans*. Philadelphia: Mason Crest, 2003.

Zannos, Susan. *César Chávez: A Real-Life Reader Biography*. Bear, Del.: Mitchell Lane, 1998.

Web Sites

Visit our Web page for lots of links about César Chávez:
http://www.childsworld.com/links.html

Note to parents, teachers, and librarians: We routinely monitor our Web links to make sure they're safe, active sites.

Sources Used by the Author

Acuna, Rudolfo. *Occupied America: A History of Chicanos*. New York: Prentice Hall, 1987.

Del Castillo, Richard Griswold and Richard A. Garcia. *César Chávez: A Triumph of Spirit*. Norman, Okla.: University of Oklahoma Press, 1995.

Levy, Jacques E. *César Chávez: Autobiography of La Causa*. New York: W. W. Norton, 1975.